10.0

The **Nadia Comaneci** STORY

10.0

The
Nadia Comaneci
STORY

By Ellen Aim

GymnStars Volume 7

Creative Media Publishing

CREATIVE MEDIA, INC.
PO Box 6270
Whittier, California 90609-6270
United States of America

www.creativemedia.net

Book & cover design by Joseph Dzidrums

First Edition: February 2016

Library of Congress Control Number
On File

Print ISBN	eBook ISBN
978-1-938438-49-3	978-1-938438-50-9

This book is dedicated to every athlete striving for perfection.

Table of Contents

"Probably, I would have been good in any sport. I was just lucky to have a gymnastics school next to the place where I was born."

How important are sports to you? Do you enjoy playing sports at school or in your neighborhood? Do you enjoy watching competitive sporting events on TV with your friends and family while you all cheer on your favorite athletes? Maybe you choose not to play sports altogether. No one is good at any sport the first few times they try it, but the only difference between an average kid and an Olympic gold medalist is practice, practice, practice!

Whether you're watching professional sports on TV or cheering on your favorite team from the stands, few things on this earth can make someone so excited, passionate, and motivated than competitive sports. That moment when the team you grew up watching wins the championship, you cannot help but feel like it was a major victory for you, as well.

Have you ever played a game of baseball with your friends and, just as you step up to bat, you picture yourself as Babe Ruth or Bryce Harper, ready to knock the ball out of the park? Maybe you play basketball, and you imagine that you are Michael Jordan or Stephen Curry when you attempt a slam dunk. If you enjoy tennis, you might pretend you are Venus or

Serena Williams when you backhand the tennis ball across the court.

No matter the sport you enjoy most, it is important to have an idol. It is inspiring to have someone you can admire and who motivates you to train as hard as you possibly can. Who knows? Maybe one day, you will beat all of the records that your idol holds. Trailblazing athletes break records that no one thought was possible. By learning from the most successful people in the world can we become the most successful people in the world.

Professional athletes need fans just as much as fans need professional athletes. When things look rough for athletes and they are in a pinch, it is the enthusiastic cheering from their dedicated fans that gives them the courage to overcome any obstacle. That is the same reason we look up to professional athletes. Their stories inspire us; their strength empowers us, and their skills and commitment to their sport is what motivates us to keep going.

For people of all ages, from Romania to Oklahoma, Nadia Comaneci is a tremendous inspiration. Among her numerous achievements, she is most famous for winning three gold medals, five total, at the 1976 Montreal Olympics. After that history-making turn, she snatched two gold and two silver medals at the 1980 Moscow Olympics. As the first gymnast to score a perfect 10 in any Olympic event, the tiny

Romanian with the soulful, brown eyes inspired millions around the globe.

Nadia believed that the only way to achieve success was through hard work, but her victories were not solely because she trained tirelessly since age six. Her outlook on life, on and off the mat, is what drove her to improve continuously as an athlete and as a human being. Even after winning titles that no other gymnast held, Nadia still looked for different ways to improve her gymnastics routine.

However, it is much more than her professional victories that made Nadia Comaneci a perfect 10. As we will see in the course of this book, she inspired greatness in everyone around her. The talented gymnast believed that surrounding herself with positive, productive people provided one of the keys to success in life.

Nadia Comaneci is still as relevant today as she was in 1976. Along with her husband, 1984 Olympic gold medalist, Bart Conner, she has created many charities and helps run a top-selling gymnastics magazine

A children's biography, *10.0: The Nadia Comaneci Story* chronicles the gymnastic legend's diverse life. Readers will enjoy learning about her childhood days in Romania, her rise to gymnastics fame, and an update on the victories that Nadia still achieves today.

"My family was very dedicated to their work. I learned from my father that the only way you achieve in life is if you put in some extra amount of work."

What influenced Nadia's indomitable spirit and commitment to her craft that transformed her into the world's most well-known gymnast?

Nadia Elena Comaneci was born in Onesti, Romania, where she lived with her mother, Stefania-Alexandrina Comaneci, a factory worker, and father, Gheorghe Comaneci, a car mechanic, and little brother, Adrian, who was four years younger than Nadia. Stefania-Alexandrina named her daughter after the female protagonist in a Russian movie that she saw when she was expecting Nadia.

Nadia means "hope." It's a fitting name for her because for weeks following Nadia's birth, doctors were unsure if the girl would survive long enough to leave the hospital. For days, her parents prepared for the worst.

Nadia was born with a rare, enormous birth defect, a fluid-filled sac on top of her head. Doctors were baffled about how how to treat the issue. If baby Nadia underwent surgery, she might not have survived, or she could have been left severely mentally handicapped afterward. Thankfully, the growth eventually disappeared without explanation.

Nadia was not too flexible, but she was powerful and resolute. She loved physical activities like playing with friends on Onesti's streets, climbing on everything, and jumping on things. Young Nadia even broke four of her parent's couches by running and jumping on them.

Looking at Nadia's long career comprised of grand achievements, it is little surprise that she started gymnastics at a young age. Nadia began gymnastics as a kindergartener with a local team called Flacara, which translates to "Flame."

The squad ignited Nadia's passion for gymnastics. Thankfully that love would burn brightly for the rest of her life.

When Nadia was just six years old, coach Bela Karolyi selected the youngster for his experimental gymnastics school after he spotted her and a friend, Viorica Dumitru, doing cartwheels at school. Bela needed female gymnasts that he could develop and train from a very young age. When the recess bell rang, all of the kids returned to class, and Bela searched every classroom until he located Nadia and Viorica. When the determined man finally found the two girls, he told them about his gymnastics class and asked to meet their parents.

Young Nadia

Nadia was ecstatic and couldn't wait to start practice sessions at Bela's gymnastics school. In 1968, when Nadia turned seven years old, she began training with Bela at one of Onesti's first gymnastics schools. From the very beginning of Nadia's gymnastic career, she trained tirelessly.

Despite the hard work, Nadia enjoyed training wih Bela. He was tough but never cruel to her. The astute coach had a knack for learning his students' personalities and adjusting their training to fit it. As a result, most of his students flourished under his guidance.

Although Nadia spent much of her time in the gym, she still contained large bursts of energy. Whenever the unabashed tomboy had free time, she perferred spending it by enjoying some form of physical activity. She loved climbing trees and swinging from the branches. Nadia also loved other sports besides gymnastics. She often played soccer with the boys in her neighborhood. On her quieter days, the aspiring gymnast went fishing with her beloved grandmother.

Undoubtedly, the all-around competition is gymnastics most esteemed title. In the four-round event, gymnasts compete in every event: vault, uneven bars, floor exercise and balance beam. At the end of the competition, the marks from all four events are added up. The gymnast with the highest overall score wins the distinction of being the best all-around gymnast.

In 1969, when Nadia turned eight, the youngster entered her first Romanian National Championships and placed 13th in the all-around event. Before her first event, her balance beam coach, Marta Karolyi, Bela's wife abd business partner, reminded Nadia to concentrate and stay focused.

The young girl wanted to make Bela and Marta so happy that she lost concentration on that apparatus and fell twice. Nadia felt so devastated and angry by her mistakes that she vowed never to make multiple mistakes again.

Although she was quite young, Bela was equally hard on Nadia. He gave his star pupil a doll as a reminder that she should never place 13th again, as the unlucky number would bring her bad luck for her entire gymnastics career. From that day forward, Nadia competed in hundreds of gymnastics competitions and never came in 13th place again. If there was anything the young girl craved most, it was a challenge.

Nearly every single day in the gym, as Nadia trained, she thought of her idol, Lyudmila Turischeva from the Soviet Union. Lyudmila was a two-time world and European all-around champion. More impressively, she had defeated the hugely popular Olga

Korbut for the all-around gold medal at the 1972 Olympics. Nadia admired Lyudmila's calm competitive attitude, her beautiful gymnastics, and her gracious sportsmanship. One day, Nadia hoped she would be as good as her hero.

The following year, Nadia began competing with the Onesti gymnastics team. At Romanian nationals, she set the record for the youngest gymnast ever to win the event. Even better, the thrilled competitor won the event in front of her hometown.

In 1971, Nadia competed in her first ever international competition, a dual junior meet between Romania and Yugoslavia. She notched her first all-around victory and contributed huge marks to her team's gold-medal victory.

Over the next few years, Nadia competed as a junior in competitions all throughout Romania and established herself as a constant medal threat. She represented Romania in dual meets with countries like Hungary, Italy, Poland, and many more, winning most of her competitions. In 1973, when Nadia turned 11, she won the all-around gold, in addition to the vault and uneven bars title, at the Junior Friendship Tournament.

At age 13, Nadia won her first major international event at the 1975 European Championships in Skien,

Norway. During the prestigious competition, Nadia captured the all-around gold medal with dominant performances. She also scored victories on the vault, balance beam, and uneven bars. The strong competitor even captured a silver medal on the floor exercise.

Nadia's success at Europeans was especially noteworthy because she had defeated her idol, Lyudmila Turischeva. As Nadia stood on the sidelines, she watched as her hero approached her. The young girl wondered if Lyudmila planned to say something to her. If so, how? They did not share a common language. Instead, Lyudmila gave the young champion a kiss on the cheek. Nadia was touched by the gracious gesture. It only confirmed her belief that Lyudmila was a class act.

That year, Nadia swept nearly every gymnastics competition she entered, winning the all-around gold at the Champions All event. Continuing a terrific season, she took first in the vault, beam, and bars at the Romanian National Gymnastics Championships. That same year, Nadia entered Montreal's pre-Olympic test competition. Establishing a high standard, she won the all-around and the balance beam event. She also claimed silver medals behind her rival, Soviet gymnast Nellie Kim, on the vault, floor exercise, and uneven bars.

In March 1976, Nadia competed in the first-ever American Cup at New York City's Madison Square Garden. At the esteemed event, she received an unprecedented perfect score of 10. Her flawless routine on the vault in both the preliminary and final rounds of competition won her the all-around gold. Incidentally, future husband, Bart Conner, won's the men's event for the United States. It was an especially sweet victory for him because it occurred on his 25th birthday.

A rumbling of excitement and awe filtered through the gymnastics community when Nadia continued earning perfect scores. Most notably, the young girl also received 10s at Japan's Chunichi Cup, where she received perfect marks on the vault and uneven bars.

Soon, the entire sports world took notice of Nadia. Gymnastics audiences roared loudly for her whenever she appeared at competitions. Before the teenager knew it, she had catapulted from Olympic hopeful to Olympic favorite.

Pensive Nadia

"Bela used to say, 'Today, we're going to do five routines on beam,' and I used to do seven."

Nadia's victories early in her gymnastics career made her a gold medal frontrunner at the 1976 Olympics in Montreal, Quebec, Canada. Despite being one of the youngest competitors at the games, Nadia's hard work, precise technique and extensive training gave her tremendous confidence against veterans, like Olga Korbut.

At age 14, Nadia became the breakout star of the Montreal Olympics. This accomplishment was no small feat in a sporting event that featured megastars, such as decathlete Bruce Jenner and boxer Sugar Ray Leonard. Yet, the tiny Romanian with big, brown eyes, and even bigger gymnastics, simply captivated the world.

During the preliminary team competition, Nadia walked to the uneven bars for her turn at the apparatus. She loved the bars and always felt like like a tiny bird flying from one bar to another. Meanwhile, gymnastics fans loved watching her.

"This could be the highlight of the compulsory event," American commentator, Cathy Rigby, remarked. "She is one of the technically best gymnasts that I've ever seen."

The youngster did not disappoint. She soared through a thrilling, somewhat dangerous, program with impeccable technique. When she completed an electrifying dismount, the crowd showered her with a standing ovation.

Equally impressed, judges rewarded her uneven bars routine with a perfect ten. At first, confusion set in among spectators and viewers at home as the Olympic scoreboard displayed a 1.00. A stunned Nadia truly believed that she had received such a low score. Fortunately, Bela conferred with the judges who explained that the score was actually a 10.0! The scoreboard was not equipped to display four numbers since no one had ever scored a perfect mark.

The spectators in attendance roared with excitement. Although the competition had not yet ended, they continued cheering for Nadia until she ran to the center of the arena for a well-deserved curtain call.

The historic score brought Nadia great fanfare. It marked the first time in Olympic history that a gymnast had earned a perfect score. The monumental achievement would be played over and over again on television highlights. The perfect moment is still often replayed even today

"Ten was the highest score, and they gave it me," Nadia smiled when she recalled the event several years later.

Throughout the Olympics, Nadia garnered six more perfect tens while capturing the all-around, balance beam, and bars titles. Plus, she won a bronze medal for a thrilling floor exercise routine. The Romanians also placed second in the team competition behind the Soviet Union. Nadia left Canada with five medals overall. She also entered the record books as Romania's first Olympic all-around champion and the youngest Olympic all-around champion ever.

Nadia's Olympic triumphs made her a household name all over the world. The instrumental song from the soundtrack of the 1971 film, *Bless the Beasts and Children*, "Cotton's Dream," became associated with Nadia after director Robert Riger used the song in a tribute video of her that aired on *ABC's Wide World Of Sports*. The haunting tune skyrocketed to the *Billboard* chart's top ten. As a result of the song's unexpected success, composers, Barry De Vorzon and Perry Botkin, Jr., renamed the song "Nadia's Theme."

"I started watching the American soap opera *The Young and the Restless* because it used "Nadia's Theme," she once recalled with laughter.

Nadia also toured the United States in an exhibition-style entertainment show called *The Nadia Tour*. The multi-city extravaganza featured many of gymnastics top stars, including Bart Conner.

Nadia was stunned by the large audiences that showed up at the performances. It was clear that the world had become infatuated with the young Romanian who made perfection look so simple. When Nadia signed autographs for people, the crowd often became unruly. Some people even reached out to touch her ponytail.

"Nadia's Theme," her own tour and wild fan fervor signaled the overwhelming truth. Romania's pride and joy had become one of the biggest celebrities in the world.

Golden Girl

"I'm not looking for the easy way to do things, and I'm proud about that."

Even though Nadia stole hearts, reached perfection, and demolished records at the 1976 Olympics, she never became complacent. Never fully satisfied, the determined athlete trained harder and harder with each day, even though her newfound celebrity required her attendance at government functions and other events.

In 1977 in Prague, Nadia successfully defended her European all-around title and scored another gold medal on the uneven bars. She initially tied Nellie Kim for first place on the vault. However, as Nadia made her way to the podium, the scoreboard reposted the final standings to give Nellie the gold alone, and Nadia won the silver medal.

Angry at what they deemed unfair judging, the Romanian government ordered their team to withdraw from the competition and return home. Although Nadia wanted to finish the event, she had to obey her country, so she left with her team.

After Nadia's team returned from Europeans, the Romanian Gymnastics Federation separated Nadia from her longtime coach, Bela Karolyi. They sent

Nadia to Romania's capital, Bucharest, to train at the Stadionul 23 August complex.

Nadia resisted the change. She already felt enormous stress from her parents' recent divorce, so losing her valuable coach, while being thrown into a new training environment, greatly upset her. As a result, her gymnastics and overall fitness suffered.

Nadia arrived at the 1978 World Championships in Strasbourg looking unfit and undertrained. She had also recently endured a growth spurt that hindered some elements. The Olympic champion finished a surprising fourth place in the all-around competition when she fell from the uneven bars. Nevertheless, Nadia did earn the world title on balance beam and a vault silver medal.

After her disappointing finish at worlds, Nadia received permission to resume working with Bela. The relieved gymnast felt overjoyed to reunite with her coach. She began training again with a renewed enthusiasm. When the champion's depression lifted, her health also improved, and she shed several pounds that she had gained. Before long, the stubborn, competitive nature returned to her dark eyes.

In 1979, a refreshed Nadia traveled to Copenhagen, Denmark, for the European Championships. In the end, the Olympic legend held off her younger teammate, Emilia Eberle, to capture her third consecutive European all-around title. Nadia became the first gymnast to achieve a three-peat in the event.

At the 1979 World Championships, Nadia led the entire women's field with 39.5 points after the team compulsories event. Unfortunately, she became ill from blood poisoning due to a cut on her wrist from her metal grip buckle. Doctors hospitalized Nadia and ordered her to rest. However, the resolute athlete left the hospital, returned to the competition, and completed her balance beam routine in the team finals. Her whopping 9.95 score gave the Romanians their first team gold medal.

After her performance, Nadia underwent minor surgery for her infected hand, which had developed an abscess. Although disregarding the doctor's orders might have hurt Nadia in the long run, she could not sit in a hospital bed while her teammates needed her. That selfless act showed her true indomitable spirit and an unwavering commitment to teamwork. Even with an injured wrist, Nadia still scored a 9.95 on the balance beam. The amazing result also illustrated her exceptional technical skills.

For her next big event, Nadia participated in the 1980 Moscow Olympics, where she finished second in the all-around event. Nonetheless, she successfully defended her Olympic balance beam title and tied with Nellie Kim for the floor exercise gold medal. Meanwhile, Romania finished second in the team competition.

Nadia left her second Olympics with four medals in all. With her combined hardware from Montreal and Moscow, the talented athlete owned a staggering nine Olympic medals.

In 1981, Nadia officially retired from competitive gymnastics. Her announcement was met with the respect she had earned through her achievements and strong sportsmanship. The International Olympic Committee chairperson and thousands of fans attended her retirement ceremony in Bucharest.

1980 Moscow Olympics

"[Defecting from Romania] was difficult because I had to leave my family behind."

Life looked fantastic for Nadia after her victory at the 1980 Olympics. Sadly, it quickly took a turn for the worst. Communist Romania was in a constant state of turmoil and its citizens felt restless.

After retiring from competition, Nadia participated in a U.S. gymnastics exhibition. During the tour, her coaches, Bela and Marta Karolyi, along with the Romanian team choreographer, Géza Pozsár, all defected to America. When one defects, they leave their country to live in another country.

Nadia felt devastated to lose Bela. Part of her felt angry and betrayed, but the other part worried for him - and herself, for that matter. The despondent gymnast wondered if she would ever see her coach again.

"It was hard," she told *ABC*. "What can you do? It was very sad."

After her return to Romania, government officials strictly monitored Nadia's actions. They worried that she would flee the country, as her coach did. When she attended the 1984 Los Angeles Olympics, officials supervised her all the time to ensure she would not defect. Aside from specially selected trips, Nadia was forbidden to leave Romania. She felt like a prisoner in her country.

At the same time, Nadia began attending university classes in Romania. She was happy to blend in with the other students and form friendships with people who knew little about gymnastics. Unfortunately, the athlete realized that the Romanian police, still fearful she would leave her country, always monitored her closely.

Finally, Nadia decided that she, too, must leave Romania. She hoped to live somewhere in North America, where she would have the freedom to make her own decisions without the government interferring in her life.

On the night of November 27, 1989, a few weeks before the Romanian Revolution, Nadia defected with a group of other young Romanians. Only her brother knew of her decision ahead of time.

In an interview with *The Daily Mail UK*, Nadia expressed her feelings the night she left Romania. "It was hard that night," she admitted. "I thought I was never going to see my family again."

Leaving Romania was the most difficult challenge that Nadia had ever faced in her entire life. However, just like all of the struggles that she overcame, she had to conquer it to advance to the next stage of her life.

Romanian Flag

Upon arriving in North America, Nadia reached out to Bela for help. He found her a temporary home in Montreal, Canada, with his Romanian friend, rugby coach, Alexandru Stefu, Once Nadia settled into life in Montreal, she immersed herself in her sport. She spent her time touring, making promotional appearances, and working as a model.

On June 29, 2001, Nadia became a naturalized citizen of the United States. Meanwhile, she also retained her Romanian passport which gave her dual citizenship. Shortly after Nadia had defected, a revolution successfully overthrew the Romania government. Many credit Nadia's defection as the final straw that made people finally fight back against the oppressive government.

*"Bart and I were friends first.
It took us about four
or five years to date."*

Nadia and her husband, Bart Conner, were made for each other. For starters, they were both Olympic gold-medal winning gymnasts who fell in love with their sport at an early age. The all-star athletes crossed paths time and time again before they eventually became husband and wife.

Nadia and Bart actually met for the first time at the 1976 American Cup in New York. The inaugural event served as a tune-up for the Montreal Olympics. When they both won their respective all-around competitions, Bart gave young Nadia an innocent peck on the cheek as part of a photo opportunity.

The two gymnasts seemed fated to eventually fall in love. While Nadia shattered more than her fair share of records, Bart's resume was extremely impressive, too. The strong competitor won a U.S. Championship, NCAA title, the Pan-American Games, a World Championship, a World Cup title, and two Olympic gold medals.

Incidentally, although Nadia and Bart both competed at the 1976 and 1980 Olympics, they were too busy with their hectic schedules to interact much.

While Bart also participated in the 1984 Los Angeles Olympics, Nadia did not. Bart snagged two gold medals and a perfect 10 on the parallel bars during those games.

After Bart's astonishing gymnastics career ended, his Olympic success landed him several lucrative endorsements. The intelligent man invested part of his financial earnings to build a gymnastics academy back home in Norman, Oklahoma.

Like Nadia, Bart's interest in gymnastics began in elementary school when he showed a natural aptitude for acrobatic moves in gym class. As a child, Bart always tried to stand on his hands for as long as he could. During his teen years, he even had parallel bars and a pommel horse at home.

In 1976, Bart Conner had studied journalism at the University of Oklahoma and joined the school's gymnastics team. There, he earned 14 NCAA All-America honors and led his team to 2 NCAA championships.

Bart watched Nadia from afar after she defected to the United States. He felt concerned for her. The kind athlete felt he could help Nadia adjust to her new American life. On one afternoon, he convinced television producers to let him appear on *The Pat Sajak Show* on the same day Nadia was as a guest.

The former competitive gymnasts hit it off right away. They enjoyed each other's company and made one another laugh. Not surprisingly, romance soon blossomed between the two.

For an entire year, Bart and Nadia spoke on the phone nearly every day. Eventually, they began working together and discovered they made a good personal and professional team.

In 1994, Bart proposed marriage to Nadia, and she happily accepted. The ecstatic couple returned to Romania for the first time since Nadia's defection for a grand wedding. On April 27, 1996, Bart and Nadia became husband and wife. After the ceremony, which was broadcast live in Romania, the delighted duo held their reception in Bucharest at the former presidential residence. The bride and groom invited 1,500 guests to their festive celebration. Not surprisingly, Nadia looked like a vision in an ornate gown that featured a 23-foot-long train.

Meanwhile, business opportunities flourished for the blissful newlyweds. Together, Nadia, Bart and businessman, Paul Ziert, ran the popular magazine *International GYMNAST*. They also formed a company named GRIPS, Etc. a producer of gymnast grips, supports, tumbling shoes, equipment and gymnastics collectibles. Bart and Nadia were also pioneers in pairs gymnastics, a sport-art form they invented, in which they toured around the world performing lyrical routines.

On June 3, 2006, in Oklahoma City, Oklahoma, Nadia and Bart welcomed their son, Dylan Paul Conner, into the world. A tight-knit family, the blissful parents took their son with them as they traveled the globe to deliver motivational speeches, promote their charities, and appear at gymnastics events.

Nadia also began touring the country with Olympic champion swimmer Mark Spitz to promote Your Personal Best, a campaign that stresses the importance of maintaining healthy lifestyles. The Olympic legend found the work quite satisfying.

"It's never too late to do something for you," Nadia often encouraged people.

Nadia and Bart

*"I'm Romanian, and
I'm adopted by the states."*

Nadia, Bart, and Dylan now live in Oklahoma City, Oklahoma. Nadia is active in countless charities and international organizations and has a long history of giving back to the community, and the world. In 1999, she earned the esteemed distinction of being the first athlete to speak at the United Nations.

Never far from the gymnastics spotlight, Nadia serves as the honorary president of both the Romanian Gymnastics Federation and the Romanian Olympic Committee. She also hosts several gymnastics shows and competitions with Bart.

Sometimes, other people pull Nadia back into the gymnastics spotlight. For example, the athletic apparel company, Adidas, asked a young Nastia Liukin to recreate Nadia's perfect 10 uneven bars routine in an acclaimed commercial that aired during the 2004 Summer Olympics in Athens.

By now, Nadia and Bart could easily settle in a big, secluded house with their son and live off their Olympic success. Except, the two prove time and time again that they are never the type to walk away from people who are in need of help.

Today, the popular duo dedicates their lives to a wide variety of charities and causes, like Nadia Comaneci Children's Clinic, the Special Olympics, the Muscular Dystrophy Association and the Nadia Comaneci Foundation in Bucharest.

In addition, Nadia helps Bart operate The Bart Conner Gymnastics Academy in Norman, Oklahoma. With hundreds of athletes using the facility, it is one of the world's largest and most well-equipped gymnastic centers.

It's clear that Nadia is still one of the most influential voices in gymnastics history, but she also enjoys making an impact outside of the gym too. In fact, Nadia might be even busier today than when she competed full-time as a competitive gymnast!

Nadia Today

*"I'm Romanian, and
I'm adopted by the states."*

Nadia broke many records during her career. Her gymnastics contributions will never be forgotten. Her commitment to athleticism is her immortal legacy. To honor her influence and achievements, International Gymnastics Hall of Fame inducted her in 1993.

When it comes to Nadia's gymnastics legacy, it is no surprise that today's gymnasts all over the world still idolize her. Looking back on the Romanian's gymnast's career, she invented and executed many intricate moves. She also possessed impeccable, innovative and ambitious, creative skills, and displayed her trademark stoic, unflappable demeanor in competition.

Nadia became a celebrity in 1976 during the Olympics. Yet, even today, she is still a relevant pop culture icon; movies, television shows, and songs still reference her.

Nadia's life has inspired many people, but her perfect gymnastics career was only one part of that. What made Nadia so successful was her attitude. No matter what a challenge presented, or what obstacle she encountered, it was the mentality that she could conquer anything which made her score so many perfect tens.

Although Nadia no longer competes in gymnastics, she still applies the same attitude of never giving up in life. She is always the first to help her friends, family, community in any way that she can.

There is no reason why you, too, cannot make a major impact in your chosen field - or in the world in general. But, just like Nadia, it's going to take a lot of hard work and training both your mind and your body. There will always be records to break and there will always be room to improve. That is the attitude that Nadia Comaneci still has today which makes her so successful.

Essential Nadia Links

Nadia and Bart's Official Web Page
www.BartAndNadia.com

International Gymnast Magazine
www.IntlGymnast.com

The Nadia Comaneci Foundation
www.NadiaComaneci.eu

Bart and Nadia Sports Experience
www.BartAndNadiaSportsExperience.com

Grips ETC.
www.GripsEtc.com

Twitter
Twitter.com/nadiacomaneci10

Competitive Record

1980 Moscow Olympic Games
All-Around - Silver
Team - Silver
Floor Exercise -Gold
Balance Beam - Gold

1976 Montreal Olympics
All-Around – Gold
Team – Silver
Uneven Bars - Gold
Floor Exercise - Bronze
Balance Beam – Gold

1979 World Championships
Team – Gold

1978 World Championships
Team - Silver
Balance Beam – Gold
Vault - Silver

1979 European Championships
All-Around – Gold
Floor Exercise – Gold
Vault – Gold
Balance Beam – Bronze

Competitive Record

1977 European Championships

All-Around – Gold
Uneven Bars – Gold
Vault - Silver

1975 European Championships

All-Around – Gold
Uneven Bars – Gold
Vault – Gold
Floor Exercise - Silver
Balance Beam – Gold

1981 Summer Universiade

All-Around – Gold
Team – Gold
Uneven Bars – Gold
Vault – Gold
Floor Exercise - Gold

1976 American Cup

All Around - Gold

1973 Junior Friendship Tournament

All Around - Gold
Vault – Gold
Bars – Gold

Now sports fans can learn about gymnastics' greatest stars! Americans **Shawn Johnson** and **Nastia Liukin** became the darlings of the 2008 Beijing Olympics when the fearless gymnasts collected 9 medals between them. Four years later at the 2012 London Olympics, America's **Fab Five** claimed gold in the team competition. A few days later, **Gabby Douglas** added another gold medal to her collection when she became the fourth American woman in history to win the Olympic all-around title. The *GymnStars* series reveals these gymnasts' long, arduous path to Olympic glory. *Gabby Douglas: Golden Smile, Golden Triumph* received a **2012 Moonbeam Children's Book Award**.

At the 2010 Vancouver Olympics, tragic circumstances thrust **Joannie Rochette** into the spotlight when her mother died two days before the ladies short program. Joannie then captured hearts everywhere by courageously skating two moving programs to win the Olympic bronze medal. *Joannie Rochette: Canadian Ice Princess* profiles the popular figure skater's moving journey.

Meet figure skating's biggest star: **Yuna Kim**. The Korean trailblazer produced two legendary performances at the 2010 Vancouver Olympic Games to win the gold medal. *Yuna Kim: Ice Queen* uncovers the compelling story of how the beloved figure skater overcame poor training conditions, various injuries and numerous other obstacles to become world and Olympic champion.

Our **YNot Girl** series chronicles the lives and careers of the world's most famous role models. **Jennie Finch: Softball Superstar** details the California native's journey from a shy youngster to softball's most famous face. In **Kelly Clarkson: Behind Her Hazel Eyes**, young readers will find inspiration reading about the superstar's rise from a broke waitress with big dreams to becoming one of the recording industry's top musical acts. **Missy Franklin: Swimming Sensation** narrates the Colorado native's transformation from a talented swimming toddler to queen of the pool.

Theater fans first fell for **Sutton Foster** in her triumphant turn as *Thoroughly Modern Millie*. Since then the triple threat has charmed Broadway audiences by playing a writer, a princess, a movie star, a nightclub singer, and a Transylvania farm girl. Now the two-time Tony winner is conquering television in the acclaimed series *Bunheads*. A children's biography, ***Sutton Foster: Broadway Sweetheart, TV Bunhead*** details the role model's rise from a tiny ballerina to the toast of Broadway and Hollywood.

Idina Menzel's career has been "Defying Gravity" for years! With starring roles in *Wicked* and *Rent*, the Tony-winner is one of theater's most beloved performers. The powerful vocalist has also branched out in other mediums. She has filmed a recurring role on television's smash hit *Glee* and lent her talents to the Disney films, *Enchanted* and *Frozen*. A children's biography, ***Idina Menzel: Broadway Superstar*** narrates the actress' rise to fame from a Long Island wedding singer to overnight success!

Fair Youth
Emylee of Forest Springs

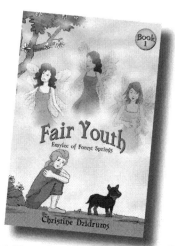

Twelve-year-old Emylee Markette has felt invisible her entire life. Then one fateful afternoon, three beautiful sisters arrive in her sleepy New England town and instantly become the most popular girls at Forest Springs Middle School. To everyone's surprise, the Fay sisters befriend Emylee and welcome her into their close-knit circle. Before long, the shy loner finds herself running with the cool crowd, joining the track team and even becoming friends with her lifelong crush.

Through it all, though, Emylee's weighed down by nagging suspicions. Why were the Fay sisters so anxious to befriend her? How do they know some of her inner thoughts? What do they truly want from her?

When Emylee eventually discovers that her new friends are secretly fairies, she finds her life turned upside down yet again and must make some life-changing decisions.

Fair Youth: Emylee of Forest Springs marks the first volume in an exciting new book series.

Ashley Moore wants to know why there's never been a girl president. Before long the inspired six-year-old creates a special, girls-only club - the **Future Presidents Club**. Meet five enthusiastic young girls who are ready to change the world. *Future Presidents Club: Girls Rule* is the first book in a series about girls making a difference!

Princess Dessabelle
Makes a Friend

Meet **Princess Dessabelle**, a spoiled, lonely princess with a quick temper.

In *Princess Dessabelle Makes a Friend,* the lonely youngster discovers the meaning of true friendship. *Princess Dessabelle: Tennis Star* finds the pampered girl learning the importance of good sportsmanship.

Quinn the Ballerina can hardly believe it's finally performance day. She's playing her first principal role in a production of *The Sleeping Beauty*.

Yet, Quinn is also nervous. Can she really dance the challenging steps? Will people believe her as a cursed princess caught in a 100-year spell?

Join Quinn as she transforms into Princess Aurora in an exciting retelling of Tchaikovsky's *The Sleeping Beauty*. Now you can relive, or experience for the first time, one of ballet's most acclaimed works as interpreted by a 9 year old.

2010 Moonbeam Children's Book Award Winner! In a series of raw journal entries written to her absentee father, a teenager chronicles her penchant for self-harm, a serious struggle with depression and an inability to vocally express her feelings.

"I play the 'What If?'" game all the time. It's a cruel, wicked game."

When free spirit Kaylee suffers a devastating loss, her personality turns dark as she struggles with depression and unresolved anger. Can Kaylee repair her broken spirit, or will she remain a changed person?

Made in the USA
Las Vegas, NV
11 March 2021

19391906R00037